A CONNOISSEUR'S GUIDE TO ANTIQUE

TOYS

A CONNOISSEUR'S GUIDE TO ANTIQUE
TOYS

RONALD PEARSALL

TODTRI

This book was designed and produced by TODTRI Book Publishers
P.O. Box 572, New York, NY 10116-0572
Fax: (212) 695-6984
e-mail: todtri@mindspring.com

Printed and bound in Singapore

ISBN 1-57717-151-9

Visit us on the web!
www.todtri.com

Author: Ronald Pearsall

Publisher: Robert M. Tod
Editor: Nicolas Wright
Art Directorr: Ron Pickless
Typesetting & DTP: Blanc Verso UK

CONTENTS

INTRODUCTION

It is often supposed that toys are things for children to play with while their elders and betters are otherwise occupied. Nothing could be further from the truth. Playing with toys is an essential skill for children, so that they can gain the necessary co-ordination of hand and mind necessary in later life and engage in social activity with their peer groups.

Many of the toys discovered from ancient civilizations make this apparent – knucklebones (jackstones) which are transferred with a flip of the wrist from the palm of the hand to the back, whipping tops where the child has to gauge when to whip and when not to, rounded stones for ball games and pebbles and marbles which act as counters for games that stimulate intellectual activity. Some games are childish equivalents of adult activities – the go-cart, often drawn by a team of donkeys, dogs, or other children, is not so different from a chariot.

Even the rattle has its place in education, teaching a baby to use its arms and hands, stimulating it by the agreeable sound. Dolls too have a role in accustoming a child to the role of mother though they do have an accessory purpose as a personal comfort. Our knowledge of early toys, as with many other forms of antiques and artefacts, derives from ancient Egypt. Toys have been discovered throughout the world, but often there is no way of knowing how old they are and how they fit in with the society of the time.

Above: A Roman terracotta chariot. Toys were not designed to have a long life and thus terracotta was often used, rather than wood or some other long-lasting material.

Opposite: With antique toys it is sometimes difficult to determine whether they are really toys or burial objects or if they serve some other purpose.

EARLY TOYS

There is always a degree of confusion with ancient dolls and whether they were toys or whether they served some religious or magical purpose. However, with most toys there is no doubt about their purpose. One of the earliest toys to be dated is a toy tiger with a hinged mouth which has been assigned to c 1000 BC, discovered at Thebes. Many such basic toys are still in use today, especially in the so-called less civilized nations.

The ancient Greek and Roman children had whistling birds, rattles in the form of ceramic animals (with a marble or stone inside), miniature carts, pull-along toys, and model horses big enough to sit on. Small animals in terra cotta, found in abundance, are not necessarily toys; dogs were a symbol of healing and therefore have a magical significance, but representations of live dogs, birds, and other creatures feature prominently on children's headstones indicating that they were probably pets. These "toy" animals, found in abundance in many different materials, were probably ornaments owned by animal-lovers and have little to do with children.

Few are sophisticated with the exception of dolls, which were often jointed in a way that did not become commonplace until the last few hundred years. They were regarded as disposable and when the children reached puberty all childish things were ceremoniously dumped. They had served their purpose. It is remarkable that they survive in any number, and presumably the ritual was frequently not adhered to or they were passed on and on to succeeding generations.

Games were frequently illustrated on vases, urns, and on wall paintings, and hide-and-seek, blind man's buff, leap-frog, and fisticuffs are all well documented. Dice and counters, and beautifully

Above: A toy on wheels from Susa (also called Sousse) in eastern Tunisia, colonised by the Phoenicians from about 1200 BC.

Opposite: A terracotta wheeled chariot from Khoveina in Syria about 2000 BC. Syria was then part of Phoenicia, the most advanced trading nation in the world with a sophisticated civilization. Military toys were very common as they made boys familiar with the art of warfare.

Left: Marbles, one of the oldest forms of toy, were also educational, teaching children co-ordination and the ability to judge distances. They were made in all materials, such as stone, clay, marble and especially glass, often multi-coloured. This selection dates from the nineteenth century.

Above: Carousel figures were very popular in America in the nineteenth century, though the giraffe is an unusual subject, the most common being the horse. America had taken the lead in adventurous toy making, many sold by mail order.

made boards, demonstrate that fairly complex board games were played, including *ludus latrunculorum*, a war game probably played more by adults than children. There are also toy soldiers in lead including Julius Caesar mounted on a horse, a precursor of the tin soldiers of the nineteenth century, though by then the initial reason was lost – to remind boys that eventually they may become soldiers.

There is no reason to suppose that during the Dark Ages toys ceased to be made, though there is little evidence of them, mostly because ritual burial was discarded and life was too hard and bitter for cast-off toys to be cherished. Children were as hard worked as adults and playing time was necessarily limited. From the twelfth century onwards small clay figures, horses, and animals exist, but the best evidence comes from illuminated manuscripts and, later, easel paintings. An English manuscript of the fourteenth century shows a boy and a man with whipping tops, and there is reference to men playing with tops in the cold weather so they would be warm and occupied in a seemly and unthreatening way.

It is surprising that more medieval wooden toys have not found their way to posterity. The Romans had almost all the carpentry tools with which we are familiar today, including the drill and the plane, and they had discovered that placing the teeth of a saw pointing alternately backwards and forwards makes the saw more efficient. It is possible that they evolved the pole-lathe, operated by using the feet, with tensed slightly flexible wood such as willow branches. Either toys such as hoops and hobby-horses have rotted away or the skills have been lost during the Dark Ages.

Cup-and-ball was a popular children's and adult pastime, so much so that Henry III of France (1551-89) took the equipment when he went out walking. Flying kites was fashionable, and there exist instructions how to make one from 1405. 1516 shows us a model jousting battle with jointed participants. As early as 1578 Nuremberg in Germany was established as a centre of toy-making when pewterers and jewelers were authorised to make tin models.

Simple toys were made by peasants in the winter months and hawked around by pedlars in the spring. Pieter Brueghel's painting *Kinderspielen* in Vienna shows many of the pastimes of the time – whipping tops, hobby-horses, hoops, skittles, marbles, knucklebones, and, probably special to the Netherlands, hand-held windmills. In Ben Jonson's play *Batholomew Fair* (1614) there is reference to various playthings on sale, such as hobby-horses, toy musical instruments, and dolls. The hobby-horse seems to have been particularly popular, the reason being that everyone rode horses and this was a simple introduction to the real thing, even if the hobby-horse was no more than a simple pole.

For the better off, toys were becoming increasingly sophisticated, and the expertise from the firearms and clock industries was used, though specific information is annoyingly sparse. In 1604 Louis XIII of France was given a clock-work pigeon as a present. He also had a model army of silver soldiers, and his collection duly passed to Louis XIV, who ordered more soldiers from Nuremberg including "automatic" ones, which might indicate that some of the soldiers were simple automata worked by clockwork.

Dolls' houses or cabinets came into being in 1558, but they were strictly adults' toys, as was the magic lantern invented about 1640. These eventually acquired a lower profile and became children's toys. Inflatable footballs were used in Elizabethan times, and rocking-horses came into being. Card games were popular, sometimes with an evangelical tinge and accompanied by an improving explanatory book.

During the eighteenth century the children of the middle and upper classes were treated as small adults and toys were frowned upon, with the exception of educational toys, one of the first of which were alphabet blocks. The

Below: The introduction of clockwork in mass-produced toys created a huge market in which the Germans were supreme. This clown on a pig and a tightrope walker of about 1900 were typical, well-made and robust. Many clockwork toys had intricate gearing and could perform astounding feats.

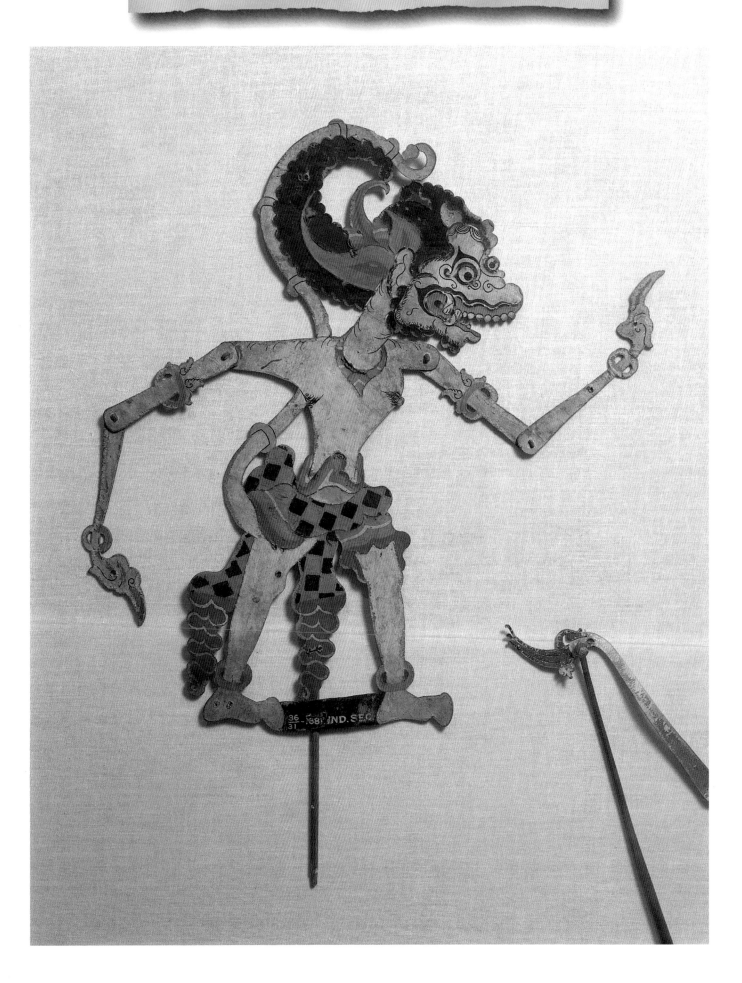

traditional toys persisted, but in 1741 there was an incredible craze, perhaps the first recorded, for the French toy the *pantin*, known in Britain as the Jumping Jack. This was a marionette operated by a single string performing a limited range of movements. It was received enthusiastically by children and adults alike (a French grand lady commissioned the painter Boucher to paint one for her), and was eventually banned by the French police in case women bore children with twisted limbs like those of the *pantin*.

It was an indication to toy-makers of the potential of new toys. Flat filigree metal toys were exported in great quantities from Germany. When made in soft alloy these could be twisted and entwined to form intricate three-dimensional figures, but from 1775 the Hilpert family of Germany poured out the staple best-seller – the flat-back soldier, as well as the flat-back civilian. Dolls, mostly directed towards the richer market, had become more lifelike, with charmingly painted wooden heads under a thin coat of gesso (plaster) ("Queen Anne" dolls) and the wax doll, an English speciality, made its appearance, owing much to the practitioners of wax figure making.

Playing cards was an important social activity in the eighteenth

Above: Three nineteenth-century chess sets, one in bone from England, and two Chinese chess sets in ivory, red and a natural colour. From earliest times chess sets could be very elaborate and were made in various materials; sometimes the sets were so convoluted that it is difficult to determine what the pieces are.

Opposite: Shadow puppets were a speciality of Java, some of which were highly elaborate and were art objects in the highly developed puppet theatre. It is still a feature of Indonesian cultural life. These are in a pierced and painted hide, and date from some time before 1881.

Above: A toy animal on wheels from Susa in Tunisia, probably of the second millenium BC though these antique objects are notoriously difficult to date precisely as they remained unaltered for centuries.

century. Hoyle's *Short Treatise on Whist* was published in 1742. He received £1000 for it, an incredible amount of money in the eighteenth century. Children too had their card games, often with a religious or instructional flavour, and this was true of the many board games. 'The New and Most Pleasant Game of Snake' was perhaps more targeted at adults, but is typical of the fare offered. For those worried about their children getting involved with dice ('the Devil's Playthings') a teetotum was substituted, a small spinning-top with flat sides or a shaped card mounted on a central axle and twirled round like a gyroscope. Jigsaws were invented in 1763 to teach geography.

In America before colonisation the same kinds of toys were used as those in Europe. Balls were made from maize leaves, rubber (solid or hollow), and stuffed animal skins. Dolls were made of wood, bone, straw, clay, wax, and other materials. Rattles and small whistles in animal shape (ocarinas) have been found in some quantity in Central and South America, as well as spinning-tops, and, rare in Europe or unrecognized, stilts.

Left: Cup-and-ball was a fashionable adult toy in the sixteenth century especially in France, amongst royalty down to the poorest. The aim was simple; catching the ball in the cup. It was a relatively short-lived craze.

Left: Children's games in the sixteenth century. Some are familiar, such as blowing bubbles and rattles, though catching the bubbles on cushions seems a strange pursuit.

The civilizations of the east coast of America took their tone from Europe, but the frontiersmen and their families often used native American toys as models for their own toys, such as corncob dolls.

In the Orient, paintings of the twelfth century depict toy pedlars and playthings including masks, kites (originally intended for the military to gauge distances), dolls, go-carts and whipping-tops, items not dissimilar to those in the west.

Nothing prepares us for the avalanche of toys that descended on the western world in the nineteenth century when children began to be regarded as creatures in their own right and not miniature adults. Before the eighteenth century, with the exception of custom-made toys for the rich, there is a painful lack of inventiveness, perhaps because the children were happy with anything, and without a demand there is no need for a supply. In the eighteenth century 80 per cent of the population lived in rural areas and most of them were poor. The children of the poor were delighted to get anything. What they did get

Above: French sailing boats in ivory from some time after 1830. They probably originated in Dieppe, the ivory-carving centre of western Europe.

Opposite: A fly-wheel-drive walking elephant from the late nineteenth century when mechanical toys began to have an important impact on what was becoming an old-fashioned industry rooted in the past.

Above: An eighteenth-century group portrait of a girl with a marmoset in a box, a girl with a triangle sitting on a magic lantern and a boy with a hurdy-gurdy. Attributed to a follower of Drouais.

were the primitive toys known to the Greeks and Romans, penny toys sold by hawkers and street vendors, and variations on ancient toys such as the peg top, a stubby cone-shaped top with a protrusion, whipped "upside down" which when freed rotated from the protrusion. In the present century there were ingenious semi-scientific cheap novelties such as the "Joey", in which a tiny phial with an open and closed end with a blob of paint on the closed end was immersed in water in a medicine bottle. By pressure on the side of the bottle the phial would submerged and when the pressure was released the phial would rise. Penny microscopes were sheets of card with a hole, on which was a blob of gum, which acted as an enlarging lens. In the 1930s and 1940s there were home-made toys such as the cotton-reel tanks, activated by an elastic band, and the match stick guns, using a length of wood, two women's hair grips, and an elastic band. By using bent hair grips and the elastic, match sticks could be "fired". This was especially popular in the East End of London.

Early toys were simple, easily understood by all nations throughout the world. They have lasted through the ages. Did the children of the Pharaohs play with skipping-ropes? It is highly probably that they did. Did the children of Rome peer through globules of gum and find that they made things appear larger? It would be surprising if they didn't.

Opposite: A somewhat gruesome "toy", a carved bone guillotine from the early nineteenth century. Previously unknown in Britain, the guillotine was brought to general notice by the French Revolution.

WOODEN TOYS

The basic material for all toys is wood, simply because it is available to all but a few civilizations. When there is little wood, as in the Australian outback, the natives find a substitute, in the case of the Aborigines cane. One of the longest established subject for toys, and ideal for carving in wood, was the horse. In the west it was the customary and usually only means of transport, and they were part of everyday life in town and country.

Toy horses have a long ancestry, ranging from stolid chunky horses on platforms, sometimes fixed, usually with four wheels, to hobby horses, and rocking horses. Many children knew that eventually they would have to ride a horse as it was the only way to get around. It was probably thought a good idea to familiarise them with horses from an early age. The hobby horse came in various guises, from a pole with a cursory cut-out cartoon-style head to a grand creation with a well-carved horse's head. The mane was usually of wool, though sometimes a real horse's mane was applied.

Games with toy horses were popular, sometimes in the form of a tournament with knights. There were also carousel tourneys where two knights rode around in a circle on hand-operated platforms and tilted at a ring suspended from a pole, a game that had a short period of popularity from the late eighteenth century. There was a revival of interest in all things knightly in 1839 with the Eglinton Tournament when a joust on a massive scale was re-created, Competitive games with horses have proved perennially attractive, and prior to World

Above: Early rocking horses were "cutouts", with two carved pieces with a seat in between, but some were very elaborate including springs to make them more realistic. This one is English from about 1840.

Opposite: A composition and wood German Jack in the Box of probably the 1830s, extremely popular throughout the century and well into the twentieth century.

War II there were numerous horse-racing games in which metal horses were propelled, or more accurately jolted, down a stretch of green fabric by turning a handle at one end.

Few hobby horses have survived, either because they were worn out or because they were hardly worth keeping. Hobby-horses are often illustrated in the nineteenth century, as by John Leech in the pages of the humorous satirical weekly magazine *Punch*, and they are usually poor things. They were given away at fairgrounds before the traditional cuddly toy.

More care was devoted to realistic horses. In 1591 a letter from a German boy requested a horse covered in goatskin from the Munich Festival, while some later ones have "proper skins". Model stables were popular in the eighteenth and nineteenth centuries along with dolls' houses, and the tiny horses are often very elegantly carved and far more convincing, and more often than not to scale, than the people inhabiting these miniature worlds. Horses on four-wheel platforms with a pram-type handle to push them are common, but there was a vogue for a platform of horses, some rearing up, and these were usually carved in Germany. Horses never lost their popularity throughout the nineteenth century, nor did the vast range of car-

Above: The child's scooter became a fashionable child's toy in the 1920s, reaching a peak in the 1930s. It could be basic, but with rubber-tyred wheels and ball-bearings round the wheel axles it was also a genuine form of transport.

Opposite: Toy cars soon followed the widespread use of real cars, and they were made of metal or wood, some of them extremely realistic and costing a lot of money. This one is a Chevrolet, probably made in France.

Above: Circus acts dating from the turn of the century, made by the renowned firm of Schoenhut & Co. from wood and papier mâché.

riages – the barouches, the landaus, the stage coaches, Hackney cabs – and these were made in all materials, very occasionally fitted with a clockwork motor. Most were initially of wood, though composition was equally suitable, and when tin-plate began to be used horse-drawn transport was nearing the end of the road, literally and figuratively. How many of these miniature carriages, often made with great skill, were toys for children is debatable. Many were made by skilled hobbyists, and there is an interesting parallel with our own age in 1953, when the coronation coach of Queen Elizabeth II was a favourite subject for home woodworkers.

Primitive horses were also made in eastern Europe, simple peasant cut-outs made acceptable by naïve and energetic decoration. The best horses were carved in Bavaria, and elephants and camels and other beasts were also done, some three feet (90 cm) tall, novelties but hardly toys and more likely drawing-room curios. Many full-length creatures carved in Germany were fixed with hooks and other attachments and set in the hall to serve as a hat and umbrella stand.

Horses on platforms were either push-along or pull-along, some had friezes concealing the wheels, and they were made in considerable numbers in Britain in the nineteenth century, some tugging wheeled wagons and carts, milk floats, water carts, coal wagons, mail vans, and omnibuses. Horses could be large enough to bear a rider – these were usually unencumbered by carriages and such-like – others could not and were merely pull-along toys, sometimes in the form of simple cut-outs that still has an appeal for young children.

There was a considerable price range. The cheapest had barrel bodies, a cut-out head, and paper decoration, the expensive ones could take a month to produce, or so the makers claimed. Horses were also made from composition, usually of the papier-mâché type but these were mainly for window display.

Today, a hobby-horse would not be recognised, or would be dismissed with scorn; not so the rocking-horse, not found very much in the present-day house but a common feature in the vestibules of supermarkets, electrically operated, and eagerly sought after by children, for whom the rocking and jerking motion is irresistible. Rocking-horse heads were often powerfully carved and belligerent in expression with fiery nostrils. A few seventeenth-century rocking-horses survive. There are two basic kinds: some rocking-horses have a boat-shaped base on which the lower body and legs of the horse were painted. Others have the legs fitted to curving planks, known as bends. Sometimes stirrups were provided.

Rocking-horses preceded rocking-chairs, introduced towards the end of the eighteenth century by, it is said, Benjamin Franklin, and the earlier ones were simple Windsor chairs with added bends. It has always been more popular in the United States than Britain, and its natural habitat is the verandah and not the sitting room. Verandahs are associated with single-storey houses, common

Below: Animals have a long pedigree, the first being Noah's Arks and their occupants, but menageries and zoos became fashionable in the nineteenth century when public zoos opened and ordinary people were able to see exotic animals. This set is American, made about 1870 by Charles M. Crandall.

Left: Painted nursery figures were very popular in the first part of the present century, either factory-produced or made by hobbyists. Nursery-rhyme figures and animals featured heavily in children's bedrooms, though Alice's Adventures in Wonderland and Through the Looking Glass with their quaint creatures such as the Mad Hatter were also mined for subjects.

in the nineteenth century in America, less common in Britain. Both verandah and bungalows are Hindi words, and the vogue for English bungalows owes much to returning servants of the Raj from India. Only in 1840 in Britain were rocking-chairs made as such, and the classic rocking-horse dates from around this period, with the bends probably made by furniture manufacturers.

Prancing horses were made, something strengthened with a metal central support, which also helped to give a centre of gravity. It was once thought that early rocking-horses had the hooves attached at the end of the rockers. This theory, amended by reference to paintings and prints, has been discarded, though there may have been such horses made by home craftsmen unskilled in theories of motion (the longer the rockers the safer the horse, though more dangerous for bystanders' feet). Real hair was often used for the mane and the tail, saddles were nailed on, though prestigious rocking-horses were fully equipped with detachable saddles and horse equippage. Children still fell off their rocking-horses and in America the Shoo-fly horse was introduced, a horse-shaped box with a seat between the two boards.

For authenticity, horses which moved up and down were invented, sometimes by strange methods, and although spring rockers are men-

Above: Skipping ropes are one of the oldest of toys, the first being made of plaited fibres, and this is a basic skipping rope with unpainted wooden handles and rope made of four twisted strands dating from about 1912.

Opposite: A high-quality swinged-platform rocking horses with realistic hide and fittings, and with the hooves carved, a sign of some distinction.

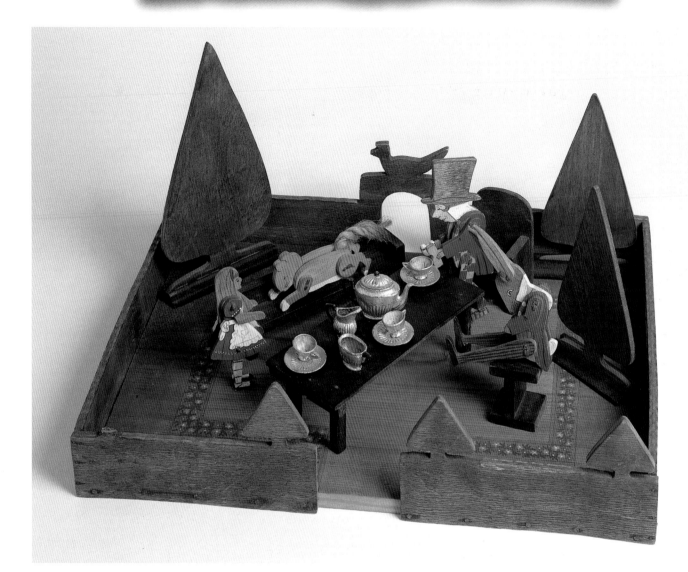

Above: An Alice in Wonderland wooden playset of the earlier part of the present century.

Opposite: The hobby horse was the precursor of the rocking horse and was considerably less fun. They could be simple cut outs, or could be very elaborate, fitted up with real horse manes and leather saddles, but this one is obviously home made.

tioned in the 1870s it was not until the early years of the twentieth century that they were made in any quantity. The successor to the rocking-horse was the adaptation of the adult velocipede with the horse mounted on three wheels, dating from the mid-nineteenth century. The wheels were wood, with metal treads, but all metal spoked wheels came in about 1860, followed eventually by solid rubber tyres. As with a penny-farthing bicycle, the velocipede had pedals attached to the axle of the front wheel, direct drive without gearing, and for a child pedalling it must have been hard work, and the velocipede faded from view. For those with money to spare, rocking-horses which moved without much effort were invented in Berlin, directed along rails laid down in a room, but it was so boring a concept that no-one bothered to put it in production.

Among the main makers of wooden horses, rockers and others, was the firm of brothers George and Joseph Lines. It also made horses for fairground roundabout. The Lines used pine for the body and beech for the legs. Most rocking-horses are anonymous, any indication of the maker long worn off if ever there.

Many simple wooden toys have never been systematically recorded, and their existence would be unknown except for references in

literature, and their appearance in pictures, prints, drawings and cartoons. There were countless variations on the monkey-on-a-stick theme in which a cut-out creature makes jerky movements by pulling a string or a piece of wood. These could cost as little as a penny or so, and were often touted by urchins on city streets. During the 1851 Great Exhibition in London these boys and girls converged on the Crystal Palace to ply their wares.

Simple wooden cut-out toys motivated by hand and worked by ratchet include circular platforms peopled by bears and similar creatures which move their limbs when the platform is turned. These were never an adequate substitute for the clockwork tin toys which followed, though both are distant relations of the upper-class toy, the automaton.

The toys of the poor, who heavily outnumbered the middle and upper classes, were probably home-made or rejects from their betters, rescued from rubbish dumps, though mass production methods and the import of cheap German toys meant that even those at the bottom of the pile could afford something. In 1871 there were one and a half million servants of both sexes, and these would be given toys their

Above: Some fairly basic wooden animals from a Charles M. Crandall (USA) menagerie, complete with flag waving keeper. c. 1870.

Opposite: A minature milliners's shop from the nineteenth century in wood, cluttered in much the same way as its real life counterpart would have been.

Left: *Before the coming of the railways, the stage coach was the only means of fast travel, and it was sometimes the only glimpse country dwellers had of the out-side world. They were thus very romantic, and model and toy stage and mail coaches, such as this one in wood from the 1830s, were often made.*

Above: A Noah's Ark with 100 figures made of wood, and dating from about 1860. Germany was the centre of the Noah's Ark industry, especially the Black Forest area and whole villages were sometimes given over to their manufacture. During World War I Belgian refugees were employed making Noah's Arks (so that they did not deprive British workers of their jobs).

employers' children had tired of and these would be distributed amongst those less fortunate. From the evidence available it is apparent that the children of the very poor had to make do with what the children of the poor had always played with – crude dolls, hoops, marbles, balls, knucklebones, skipping ropes, and hopscotch, a name first mentioned in 1801.

Cut-out figures and animals, brightly painted and mounted on wheels as pull-along toys or placed on a stand, had long been produced in Germany, often labour intensive and made by families (in 1821 one toy-maker , Lang, employed more than 100 carvers). One

family of carvers specialised in six animals – dog, cat, wolf, sheep, goat, and elephant. Many of these did animals in the round, but the wood-carvers were under threat not only by the introduction of tin-plate and die-cast toys but by the invention of the jigsaw in the 1870s, which greatly reduced the time needed to cut out a figure of animal, and which could be set up to produce a piece in quantity.

In 1917 plywood was invented, and cut-outs proliferated. Any pictures of nurseries of the 1920s show cut-out figures mounted on a stand and displayed on dressing-tables and mantelpieces. The equivalent cut outs were made in pottery by such potters as Clarice Cliff. This was a time when fretwork was becoming a very popular hobby, and alongside pipe-racks and teapot stands were cut outs of all kinds, with designs provided by many magazines especially *Hobbies*. The fretwork saws were either hand-held or operated by a treadle. There were few middle-class children of the 1920s and 1930s who did not go through a fretwork phase.

The numerous animals produced in Germany from the eighteenth century were also destined for Noah's Arks, which were never considered as religious objects. These were made in immense quantities, and were really equivalents of dolls' houses with animals instead of people. They also appealed to boys as much as girls, and because they had little or no appeal to adults they were more cheerful, less obsessive, and cheaper. They could also be crammed with whatever appealed to the young owner – animals of wood, papier mâché, metal, celluloid, and plastics. The owner of Cremer's toy shop in London visited Saxony in 1875 and was aghast because insects and birds were out of scale with the elephants. He saw it as a Teutonic plan or a deliberate attempt to combat Darwinism and modern science

As many as 370 figures are found in some German arks. Sometimes the creatures are on legs, sometimes mounted on square bases. One town at Halbach in Germany had 24 firms, all devoted to the manufacture of Noah's Arks. Arks were provided with a traditional dove bearing an olive leaf fixed on the roof. Occasionally arks were as elaborate as dolls' houses with several rooms, a kitchen, and stables. It was common practice to mount the ark on a boat, which might float, but sometimes they were given wheels so that they could double as pull-along toys.

Most arks were provided with a porch and access to the interior was by a lift-off lid or a door at the back, and some arks had clock-work mechanisms so that animals would mount the steps to the ark while Noah gravely acknowledged them by raising his arm. Arks decorated by gluing straw to them are sometimes inaccurately known as prisoner-of-war ware, but they were German commercial products. All variations were tried, and all finishes, painted or covered with lithograph designs.

During World War I supplies of arks from Germany stopped, and disabled ex-servicemen filled the demand, along with the thousands of refugees who had flooded in when the war broke out. They were given arks to make as the trades unions objected to them doing practical work as it would deprive English workers of their jobs. The work of these amateurs is generally crude.

Above: The Dutch were the first to make dolls' houses, which were often superbly equipped with miniature furniture. This cabinet dates from 1743, made of walnut veneer on oak and is ascribed to Sara Loos van Amstel, who died in 1760.

Opposite: Picture bricks were a favourite Victorian toy. Often they had different pictures on each face, so there could be six different solutions. Few have survived, as the printed pictures glued to the wooden blocks have invariably peeled off in the course of time.

A near relative of arks are farms, menageries and zoos, some of them drawing-room pieces rather than toys. So many new animals were being brought back from the corners of the globes that they were a constant topic of conversation. The American Humpty Dumpty Circus made by Albert Schoenhut in 1903 brought a new level of expertise with figures with as many as six joints each, so that children could place the toys in numerous postures. It was one of the earliest American toys to be exported in quantity, and an early indication that Germany had a formidable rival in the toy-making business. Some of the figures had bisque and china heads. It was also a sign that multiple elements in a toy had long-lasting appeal, the most outstanding example of which is the train set.

Miniature wooden figures, whether of people or animals, and especially soldiers carved in enormous quantities in Saxony, were eventually to be made obsolete by William Britain's method of casting in metal, in which greater accuracy and detail could be displayed and

Above: An American toy piano by
Schoenhut & Co. of the nineteenth century.
Some toy pianos were quite elaborate, with
moveable keys striking tuned metal bars of
unequal length.

scale could be realistic. As with dolls, wooden Noah's Arks and their inhabitants could be replaced by card, and these were supplied either in boxed sets or as giveaways. Many German miniature figures and animals were made in composition, but few exist as the material has rotted away.

Among the longest lasting wooden toys are building blocks, in which cubes, oblongs, cylinders, arches and spires are assembled to make buildings. In technique they were superseded by clip-in building blocks such as Lego, but they are still enormously popular with the younger children at nursery schools and at home for whom Lego is too sophisticated. Alphabet blocks are among the most popular of simple educational toys.

Above: Toy theatres were a popular Victorian pastime and had a large spin-off amongst the toy trade, which provided cut-out card figures, paste-on bits and scenery, often pushed across the stage along slots. The key manufacturer was Pollock.

In most wooden toys a question arises which no-one has every satisfactorily answered. How is it that the natives of southern Germany were so talented in carving, talent that sometimes merges into genius? Other nations have vast tracts of forest yielding suitable wood, but nowhere is there any equivalent to these carvers, largely of humble origin, often working in their own homes for minuscule wages. There is perhaps no answer, and it is just a quirk of history. The same question could be asked of the ivory carvers of Dieppe, or the carvers of bone by French prisoners of war in Dartmoor Prison during the Napoleonic Wars (sometimes the same people). A possible answer is that those with the talent converged on the area, just as in Britain experts in the shaping of jet jewellery moved to Whitby, the centre of the industry.

With the exception of dolls and the miniature furniture designed for dolls' houses, most wooden toys were uncomplicated, though toy wooden trains were fitted with clockwork motors. Only for the traditional toys such as hoops and tops was wood the ideal material.

Above: Victorian building bricks with multi-faceted sides so as to present different pictures. They were popular in all levels of society, and in nursery schools they still are, answering the child's need to solve simple problems.

Opposite: A group of Victorian nursery furnishings including a rocking horse on a moving horizontal base, a scrapwork screen - a popular home pursuit - and a basic child's chair.

METAL TOYS

Tin-plate consists of sheets of iron and steel thinly coated with tin by being dipped in a molten bath of that metal. Its primary use is for tin cans to preserve meat, fish, and other edible products, and for the manufacture of household utensils. It was first produced in Bohemia (now part of the Czech Republic), which held a monopoly, but around 1620 the industry spread to Saxony, where it was investigated by an English engineer. Manufacturing, however, did not start in Britain until John Hanbury (1664 – 1734) devised a method in Wales, for rolling the alloy between cylinders. The use of tin-plate spread rapidly through England and Wales and Britain became the chief manufacturer. In America large-scale production did not start until about 1890.

The possibilities for making toys in tin-plate were seized by the Germans, who towards the end of the nineteenth century were on their way to becoming industrial rivals of Britain and the United States, and, with the exception of dolls, were dominating the toy market. Until the tin-plate age toy-makers were largely anonymous, but the tin-plate market was dominated by a handful of major players. The firm of Hilperts of Nuremberg, most famous for their soldiers, operated in the town from 1775. The town attracted itinerant toy-makers because of the workers' low wages and the presence of clock-makers who could easily switch over to mechanical toys. Wooden toys with clockwork mechanisms had been made for some time, but tin-plate was more suitable. The toys were so cheap that the British and the Americans could not and would not attempt to compete. In England tin-toy makers produced thousands of penny toys

Above: Carette was one of the supreme makers of clockwork toys, and this Mercedes tourer of about 1907 is characteristic of his finely finished products.

Opposite: William Britain was the most famous maker of lead toys who kept up to date with trends. His Mickey Mouse was typical of his 1920s and 1930s work.

Above: A German tinplate "carpet" train (indoor rather than outdoor) made by the renowned firm of Marklin about 1905, though in this particular genre Britain was supreme with Hornby and Bassett-Lowe, which to this day have no parallel.

Opposite: The Dinky toy was perhaps the most widespread boy's model toy of the 1930s, and cars, aircraft, and ships were modelled with great accuracy for the mass market. This is a rarity, a wooden Dinky mock-up of an unissued green "Albion" post-war milk tanker.

which were sold by vendors at Ludgate Circus in London, some of which were made in the UK.

The Germans, skilled in organization, used interchangeable parts, mass production, advanced technology (the use of electric power), and the use of scrap tin-plate to maximise production. They were also skilled in promotion with trade shows in which the toys could be seen being made. Duty on mechanical toy exports was levied on weight. This is one of the reasons why tin-plate toys were often fragile and vulnerable, their appeal lying in the surface decoration, painted, stencilled, or lithographed, the main method. It was cheap and versatile, and the decoration could be angled at the individual countries to which the toys were exported. Identical items such as ships were exported all over the world; it was necessary only to change the flag and the name of the ship.

In 1908 12,000 toy-makers were employed at Nuremberg, half of them women and girls whose wages were half those of men. One

third of the total production went to America, using commission merchants who arranged all the transactions. Because of the scale of the operation quality control was limited; at a trade fair in Leipzig in 1909, 80 per cent of the toys were faulty. Fluctuations in American demand, and the build-up of the American toy industry, made toy-making a hazardous business.

Although there were hundreds of smaller factories, the main manufacturers in Germany were the Bing Brothers, Märklin, Lehmann, and Carette. Ignaz and Adolf Bing established a factory in Nuremberg in 1865 to manufacture kitchenware, then branching out into tin toys. Märklin, founded in 1859 to make miniature kitchenware, moved to Goppingen, Germany. Lehmann was founded in Brandenburg in 1881 to make metal boxes. Carette of Nuremberg came to prominence after 1895 and built up a strong connection with the prestigious British firm Bassett Lowke, where quality not quantity was valued most.

Anything that could be made of tin-plate was made, and tin-plate "replicas" (often out of scale) of the latest models of cars, aeroplanes, ships, and aircraft were produced within a few weeks of their intro-

Above: A German Marklin painted clock-work trolley, an unusual subject, dating from the early years of the century. World war I ended the supremacy of Germany in clockwork toys and they were not fully to recover their pre-eminence.

Opposite: A selection of Alfa-Romeo racing cars of great value as the prestige cars, whether full scale or miniature, always command a premium.

Pages 50/51: The Victorians were immensely skilled at mechanical working models of industrial objects, such as pumps and engines. This one-eighth scale model of a GWR Firefly class 2 - 2 -2 locomotive made by Sir Daniel Gooch, dates from about 1845.

Left: A model German railway from about 1870. Before the advent of the motor car the train and the ship were the most common subjects for mechanical toys.

Above: A selection of mechanical toys, a Lehmann animal toy, and two mechanical banks, a J. & E. Stevens "Paddy and the Pig" and a girl in a chair, all dating from the nineteenth century .

Opposite: A large Marklin tinplate horse-drawn carriage of about 1880. The use of tin plate was one of the great inventions in toy making. It was cheap, could be mass produced.

centre one electrified. Hornby was also the inventor of "Meccano" ("Mechanics Made Easy"), perhaps the most famous of constructional toys and arguably the finest.

The best toys were "scratch" toys, accurate scale models, but these were very expensive and were hardly toys. In this field, the Americans and the British were supreme with Bassett Lowke playing a leading role. The German philosophy was "pile them high", though the leading manufacturers did produce some splendid scale models as well as submarines which look like flying saucers and ships where the ridiculously out-of-scale flag would have caused the boat bearing it to turn turtle.

The output of the German toy factories was phenomenal, and it is surprising that the toys are not around in greater quantity, though there are enough for them to form a niche in the antique market. The highest valued are those in their original boxes and in near mint condition. These command very high prices, but have always been rare as few children kept the original boxes and the tin toys were easily damaged, or at least badly scuffed.

Tin toys were also made in France, especially the firm of Martin, but even when tin toys were turning up regularly at auction in the 1970s (where the best sold between about £100 and £200), Martin toys were quite rare. French tin cars were of high quality and served as advertisements for the full-sized models. Later tin cars were fitted with genuine Michelin tyres.

The British were rather scornful of tin-plate toys, though some minor firms did produce them, owing much to the German types, and there were superior toy-makers such as Bassett Lowke and James Beeson, models rather than toys. The American tin-plate industry was more energetic, starting in Connecticut and moving to New York. One of the most famous was Edward Ives with his slogan "Ives Toys make happy boys", beginning production in 1868, when he made

dancing figures driven by hot air rising from a household stove.

As a medium, the Americans preferred cast iron to tin-plate; the marvellous range of cast-iron money boxes (widely faked) are the most famous. Despite its versatility, the lithographic method of colouring toys arrived late in America and toys of around 1900 were painted and stencilled in a way that had long gone out of fashion in Britain and Europe. Despite great advances half of all the tin toys in America in 1914 were imported, mainly from Germany.

After World War I there was a brief period when German toys were no longer popular in the United States. Eventually the Germans re-geared themselves and once more became important producers of tin-plate toys. Tin-plate was an ideal material for toys as it was cheap, it took bright colour, and so far as the manufacturers were concerned it had the advantage of being easily damaged and prone to rust, so that replacements would have to be made. The shelf-life of tin-plate was short, and tin-plate toys share the fate of tin-plate biscuits tins – unless they are in good condition they are worthless.

After World War I the United States was perhaps the most inventive in the tin-plate toy market, and cinema cartoon characters were speedily taken up, especially those with a world-wide appeal such as Mickey Mouse, Minnie Mouse, Donald Duck and Goofy. The main manufacturer was Louis Marx, born in 1894; he became a millionaire by the time he was 30, and was the largest toy-maker in the world. His "Mouse Orchestra" featured four mice grouped around a piano. A curious feature of American tin toys is the popularity of fire-

Above: A Britain's sample card with factory sample numbers under each figure, a source of great information for toy historians, for little has been systematically saved. When William Britain's toys were first produced no-one would have believed that one day they would attain the status of antiques

Opposite: A soldier guardsman, a genre which has never gone out of fashion though today replaced by Action Man and his ilk, logically a descendant of the old-fashioned toy soldier.

Above: A Mickey Mouse organ grinder. Of all the 1920s and 1930s childhood icons probably Mickey Mouse stands out from the crowd, most of the others, such as Bonzo the dog, being almost forgotten though an exception has to be made for Snow White and the Seven Dwarfs.

Opposite: Many Dinky toys can be considered subtle advertising instruments as in this Golden Shred (marmalade) van and the Heinz Tomato Ketchup van.

engines, of only limited interest to British and European children.

Tin-plate toys were popular until the 1960s, but Japan was proving to be the most enterprising when fashioning the new novelty toys – space ships, astronauts, robots, though the numerous forms of plastic were ousting metal. Plastic was more versatile, and was even cheaper to make. Action Man and gaudy tin-plate co-existed for a time. The Japanese toys are either awful or of exceptional quality. Their large-scale re-creations of American classic cars such as Cadillacs, Chevrolets, and Buicks of the 1950s are outstanding. The Japanese toys were often battery-driven, and their robots – feverishly collected by the Japanese – were technically well ahead of the competition in the west.

The children of the nineteenth century were lucky in the variety of toys available. For the offspring of the middle and upper classes it was a good time to be young, as for one of the first times in history they were looked at as individuals and not adults manqué with their own interests and preferences, even if these were sometimes over-rode by the wish to improve the young despite themselves.

At a time when wars were interesting rather than dangerous to civilians, there was great enthusiasm amongst boys in toy solders, first of all supplied in great quantity by Nuremberg, stamped out of metal and in one dimension, appropriately known as "flats". Meticulous

painting often made these cheap figures attractive. Armies were formed, often correctly rigged out in the correct uniforms, and elaborate battle games were played out in the nurseries and amongst men on the dinner table. It must not be supposed that metal soldiers ousted traditional wooden soldiers completely. In 1864 there had been 697 manufacturers of wooden toys in Saxony alone, and a good number of them survived the tin-plate onslaught. There were also paper soldiers, mostly cheap cut-outs, of marginal, if any, interest.

The best military figures and equipment were made from 1893 by the British firm of William Britain & Sons, which perfected the hollow-cast method. Although there were competitors such as Johilco and Reka, Britain provided more than half the lead soldiers produced. The craze spread to other figures and accessories, and zoos, menageries, and especially farmyard and garden scenes were peopled by a vast variety of correct-to-scale creatures and realistic accompaniments. Odds and ends from these multi-piece games frequently turn up, but complete sets in their original boxes are quite rare. They are amongst the most charming and nostalgic of 1920s and 1930s toys.

Few, if any, have pondered on the social effects of the enthusiasm for toy soldiers and war games amongst both men and boys. Generals setting out table-top strategies and tactics using toy soldiers is a cliché, but true none the less. Many volunteers of World War I went

Above: A two-seater Benz racing car of 1904 when cars first became a familiar feature on the roads.

Opposite: A pre-World War II double-decker bus. Buses were often highly detailed with destination boards, registration numbers and sometimes even passengers. They were made and sold in large quantities as for many children it was the only form of transport they ever travelled in.

Over leaf: Although it was mostly associated with trains, the firm of Hornby also produced other vehicles such as this truck and delivery van, always made to high standards. Die-cast models have stood the test of time better than tinplate toys.

Above: A between-the-wars German mechanical bank of tin plate. When the lever is depressed, the sailor stands to attention and salutes.

Opposite: Clockwork became more or less obsolete with the widespread introduction of battery electrics and electronics. Japan speedily recognised a new market, and from the 1950s they pioneered robots and space-age toys.

into what they thought was a great game. In fact some at the head of the armed forces seemed never to lose the illusion. One sometimes feels that set pieces, such as the naval Battle of Jutland, were created by fantasists who had learned their skills in the nursery.

Even more popular than die-cast soldiers were die-cast vehicles, mostly made of lead or a lead-based alloy and painted with a lead paint. They are the most widely collected of toys, but, as with tin-plate, they have to be in good condition and preferably in their original boxes. In 1934, encouraged by the great success of American "Tootsietoys" the British Meccano company produced their first "Dinky" toys, which encompassed aeroplanes and ships as well as cars, lorries, and other transport. These were made to scale, and the range was vast, including European and American models as well as British. Some of the models were very complicated, such as the Mayo-Mercury "piggy-back" plane (a large plane carrying a smaller one on top) of the 1930s. Although production ceased during World War II, demand was still high after the war. The "Dinky" toy was so profitable that there were other ventures which were almost indistinguishable, such as the "Matchbox" toys. There was no clockwork mechanism, the tyres were of rubber (which always came off and were lost). They were push-along toys, as were those of other rivals, such as Lesney which produced their "Models of Yesteryear" series, and Corgi, whose vehicles were slightly larger, had independent suspension, and a bonnet which could be lifted to reveal an engine. They were not so lively as "Dinky" toys which were all of the highest quality, and as they were all to some degree superseded by battery and electronic toys it was evident that the great age of toy-making had gone.

SCIENTIFIC TOYS

It must not be supposed that all toys were amiable playthings, demanding nothing from children excep the ability to wind things up or clothe and unclothe dolls. In the eighteenth and nineteenth centuries in particular instruction and entertainment went hand in hand and the dissemination of scientific ideas resulted in an immense range of toys used by adults and children alike. As with board and card games, they transcended the age barrier. There were few middle-class homes that did not have a microscope or a telescope, even if it was of tin-plate and had the most rudimentary of lenses.

Since the Renaissance scientific discoveries had been made at an astonishing rate, though sometimes it was difficult to use them as although the theory was there the technology was lacking. Leonardo da Vinci's notebooks are full of marvellous concepts, some of which had to wait until the

twentieth century to be utilised. There was no way in which an aeroplane could be constructed during his lifetime (1452 – 1519).

Unlike some areas of life, such as common sense, technology always progresses, and although there were always inventors of genius – Archimedes, the architects of the Middle Ages, the clock makers and makers of firearms – it was only in the seventeenth and eighteenth century that systematic efforts were made to bring science to everyone. Societies, such as the Royal Society (founded in 1660), for the propagation of science proliferated. The Royal Society had a Curator of Experiments whose duty was to provide

Above: The thaumatrope was one of the immense variety of scientific toys relying on the phenomenon of persistence of vision, and these could be simple or elaborate. The word "thaumatrope" is a portmanteau word meaning miracle and turning.

Opposite: A beautifully preserved AJH Steward tri-unial magic lantern from around 1880.

"three or four considerable experiments each day the Society met"

Robert Hooke was the first curator, and his work on the microscope and Isaac Newton's work on optics and astronomy encouraged instrument makers at the end of the seventeenth century to provide scientific instruments not only for the professionals but for the intelligent layman. King George III and the Earl of Bute built up considerable collections, as did lesser mortals. As the interest spread lectures and demonstrations were eagerly attended by children as well as adults, and the complex and sophisticated instruments were stripped of their mystery and in a cut-down form became scientific toys which

Above: During the nineteenth century many traditional toys were renamed to make them seem new. One such was the teetotum, later revamped as the repulsion. The date of this toy would be the mid 1800s.

Opposite: The autogiro was the first form of helicopter. It was sufficiently noteworthy to be reproduced as a toy. This one is by William Britain and dates from the mid-1930s.

Left: One-off models, known as "scratch" models, were produced well into the present century and are probably still being made today by enthusiasts. This is a 1928 scale model of a Burrell three-shaft traction engine, finely engineered and fully equipped, made by D. J. Moir

Above: Leonardo da Vinci (1452 - 1519) invented a whole host of objects, including a flying machine, but there was no technology available for making them. This sketch of a flying machine, though improbable by modern standards, must be fitted into the context of the time.

Opposite: A Bing stationary steam engine of about 1902 and a Carette car of slightly later date.

not only made abstruse theories understandable but were fun to use as well. A typical example was the gyroscope, which basically uses the same principle as a whipping top, and which was popular until the present day. Many of the scientific principles on which toys were based were instinctively understood, and they could be explained in simple terms without reference to frightening terms such as physics, mechanics and optics.

Science was also stimulated by numerous books many directed at children, and although *Philosophical Recreations, or Winter Amusements: A Collection of Entertaining & Surprising Experiments* of the early nineteenth century when science-for-all really began to get under way in a serious manner would have been a tough nut to crack for a youngster, there were no such reservations about *The Boy's Playbook of Science, Through Magic Glasses*, and *The Fairyland of Science*. Many of the devices were known and appreciated by the ignorant and poor, such as the magic lantern, and the audiences at lecture-demonstrations were often terror-stricken by the "dissolving views" where slides were superimposed or were jiggled about by simple mechanisms. They were also scared by lantern-slide lectures on the "Evils of Drink", a popular subject in slum-based halls, which usually portrayed science-fiction-type bugs as prime constituents of alcohol. The first magic lantern made for children was produced in 1843.

One of the longest-lasting of scientific toys was the chemistry set, which was first advertised about 1840. Children were encouraged to take an interest in natural history and the collecting of plants, shells, and stones was a widespread hobby, and there were a number of accessories available such as small chests to keep the collection in, as well as geological hammers. Such hobbies benefited other industries like mapmakers and writers of handbooks, who, thanks to the invention of new colour processes such as lithography, could produce full-colour books cheaply. Astronomy was also popular and as well as cheap low-power telescopes, orreries (mechanical constructions to portray the movement

of the planets round the sun) were made for children.

Strictly speaking, spinning tops, yo-yos and hoops are scientific toys (inertial devices depending on the conservation of movement). The yo-yo is of great antiquity and enjoyed a vogue in the Regency period when they were sometimes made of ivory. The yo-yo was rediscovered in 1932, when it was given its name. Its earlier name was bandalore. Another inertial toy is the diabolo (a double cone rotated by a string held between two sticks), known as "the devil on two sticks" which was described in an 1820 book of juvenile games. It is a cross between a whipping top and a yo-yo.

The force of gravity was often used in penny toys, and tumblers or toy acrobats were often fitted out with lead weights or partly filled with mercury, the mysterious metal in liquid form. The principle of the lever was used in pecking birds, which had a pendulum beneath a base board.

Centrifugal force was used in a hoop made of two parallel wires, between which a ball was swung round without falling off. Many children were amazed by objects moving on a board apparently on their own. They were activated by a magnet moved under the board.

Above: A pre-World War I bagatelle player made in Germany, the balls being returned to the player by means of an Archimedean screw. These types of games, particularly horse-racing games, were very popular, a trend that continued to the end of World War II when more sophisticated pastimes and toys came into existence.

Opposite: A Marklin tinplate sand mill diorama, an unusual and not, one would have thought, very commercial when compared with toys, trains and mechanical novelties.

Right: The skeleton mechanism of a mechanical Scotsman made about the 1880s, though toys of this period are notoriously difficult to date within a few years. One of the few clues is from advertising or catalogues. Only a limited number of manufacturers marked their products in the nineteenth century.

Above: The line between automata and toys is very tenuous, and the difference between them mainly lies in the ages of the owners. This mechanical spider of the highest quality is made in silver, steel and brass, possibly Swiss, as the early makers of automata were principally watch makers who flourished in Switzerland.

Below: A catalogue page of model mechanical toys including animals, engines and figures of 1880, sold by mail order in America. The full catalogue contained 700 illustrations and even considering the impact of time there are surprisingly few remaining, and those that do are eagerly collected.

Artificial magnets had been made in the eighteenth century using powdered manganese or iron, though magnetic force and the lodestone had been used since the twelfth century in the west though magnetism was known to the adventurous sea-faring Arabs before then. A simple magnet-based toy was a box containing tiny metal fishes; these were fished for by a small magnet at the end of a fishing-line. Small magnets were not strong enough to be utilised in any sophisticated manner, and electro-magnets were too large for toys.

Static electricity was also used, and although the parents had to turn the handle of the glass friction machine it was the children who were delighted by dancing puppets made of pith, and dolls whose hair stood up. Although the electric dynamo was invented by Michael Faraday in the 1830s it could not be used to any great extent, though tiny electric dynamos powered by small steam engines could generate enough power to light up a small bulb. Although electric motors were used in model trains in the 1890s it was not until the 1930s that the full possibilities were realised.

There were a number of toys, especially divers and boats powered by camphor pellets. Motion resulted from the surface tension of the water/camphor mix. These are distinct from the vessels powered by methylated spirits. But of all the scientific toys the most popular and important were the optical toy. These had an enduring appeal for children and adults alike, the magic lanterns, the camera obscura (a box with a pin-hole

and a ground-glass screen on which the inverted image of the outside scene was projected), and the stereoscope, where two photographs glued on card placed side by side merged into a three-dimensional single image when looked at through a pair of lenses. In 1861 the stereotrope was invented in which eight pairs of stereoscopic photographs were mounted on the outside of an octagonal drum and viewed through a stereoscope. A shutter prevented the viewer seeing the pair of photographs in motion. The purpose of this instrument is not clear, as it is merely an easy way of viewing stereoscopic photographs without the trouble of spending a couple of seconds changing ordinary stereoscopic images on their stand.

A kaleidoscope was a tube that presented always changing geometric shapes to the viewer holding the tube to his or her eye, relying on cleverly sited mirrors. Photographs were sometimes used. High quality kaleidoscopes had a turning mechanism but most were simply shaken. Mirrors fascinated the Victorians, as they do today; perhaps the distorting mirrors of old time funfairs are somewhat *demodé* but they have their devotees. A curious off-shoot of the distorting mirror was a device in which distorted drawings were reflected in a metal mirror and seemed perfect.

Many of the nineteenth-century optical toys relied on the phenomenon of persistence of vision. Most of them were given long and unpronounceable Greek names. The thaumatrope invented in 1825 was the simplest of devices, a circular card with a picture of a bird on one side and a picture of a cage on the other. When twirled between the fingers, the bird appeared to be in the cage. The phenakistoscope of 1832 and the zoetrope, also known as the "Wheel of Life", of 1860 belong to the same family. In these a series of drawings is viewed through slits in a rotating disc or drum, and an impression of movement is captured. A galloping horse was a favourite theme. A more sophisticated model was the praxinoscope of 1877 in which mirrors were incorporated. There was a mirror for each image and there was a great improvement in the light that could be brought to bear. The cheapest and most common toy to use persistence of vision are the flip-books, in which the pages of a small book each with a slightly modified drawing of the previous drawing are flicked through using the thumb so that the different drawings make a moving picture – the same principle used in the pre-computer age by Walt Disney and other film cartoon makers.

The zoogyroscope uses a series of time-lapse photographs set side by side inside the rim of a disc or drum, viewed through a slit, made possible by the work of the photographer Muybridge who filmed a galloping horse by having it gallop past a line-up of 40 cameras. His naked men and women running or gambolling past the cameras had, and maybe still have, an esoteric appeal to collectors of erotica. Without these clever toys the advent of cinematography may have been delayed. The images on a reel of film stock are not so remote from the Muybridge experiments in animal and human motion.

Historically the most important of the optical amusements was the magic lantern, and endless efforts were made to get animation. Superimposition, complete or in part, was the easiest, so that a woman's hat could fly off, or a head could nod, or an ugly face could

Left: Spinning tops are known throughout the ancient world, both in the sophisticated world of Europe and amongst the widely spaced ethnic communities, and they continue to hold their appeal, though today's tops are more sophisticated, with optical and sound effects, though the traditional humming top is long established.

Above: A Humpty Dumpty circus relying on the time-honoured popularity of nursery-rhyme characters.

Right: Horse-racing games were adult toys in the late nineteenth century and worked on a variety of principles. The most expensive in the Ascot range was £4. 4. 0., nearly a month's wages for a labourer.

turn into a beautiful face. The slides were normally of glass, though celluloid was occasionally used. Lighting varied, and the means included petrol, methylated spirits, gas, acetyline, and, later, electricity. The quality of the slides ranged from the amateurish and infantile to the splendid, the work of true artists. The magic lantern was the ancestor of the slide projector, and they have one thing in common for the viewer – sitting in a darkened room hoping against hope that the show would not go on too long.

Opposite: Toy makers speedily took advantage of current events and as most were small businesses this could be done almost overnight. Typical of the novelties was the Crystal Palace peep show ("Lane's Telescopic View"), invented soon after the Crystal Palace was opened in 1851.

Left: A collection of low-cost toys, sometimes no more than a penny, including a wind up gramophone, a monkey up a pole, and a pea-shooting battleship.

DOLLS

The earliest dolls that can definitely be called dolls rather than religious or magical figurines date from ancient Egypt. They were made in all materials, as were the dolls in ancient Rome and Greece, where there were elaborate joints and a level of skill rare before the eighteenth century except perhaps in Germany where there was a long tradition of carving religious figures. Crèche figures for Nativity and other religious themes could be newly interpreted as dolls.

Most of the early dolls were of wood or fabric, bone or ivory. Many were home-made, though peasants carved wooden dolls throughout the long winter evenings, selling them door to door in the spring or supplying itinerant pedlars. Rag dolls were probably mostly made in the home by mothers and sisters, and those few that have survived are found to have several overlaid faces; as soon as one wore out another was sewn on.

Although primitive dolls were found beneath paving stones in Nuremberg, little exists prior to about 1750, and wooden figures such Lord and Lady Clapham, made in the middle of the eighteenth century, are extraordinarily rare. They are well-carved, but in posture and expression stiff and staid. Such dolls are known as Queen Anne dolls for no very clear reason. The heads are often primed with gesso (plaster of Paris) and skilfully painted on that.

The best dolls came from southern Germany and with the increasing communication between countries, quantities of German wooden dolls, known as Grödnertals after the region where they were made,

A piano doll by J. Secor, designed, as the name suggests, to be ornaments to be placed on the tops of pianos and not children's playthings.

Opposite: A group of Teddy bears and soft toys. Soft toys of one kind or another, such as rag dolls, have existed since earliest times, but the Teddy bear was named after US president Theodore Roosevelt early this century.

Above: A high-quality Georgian-type doll's house made about 1810. Many were furnished with no expense spared and they have enjoyed a continuing vogue amongst adults.

Opposite: Pedlar dolls came in a vast variety, often with accessories, such as baskets of flowers while some were part of tableaux representing market stalls. They were originally sold at fairs and made by itinerant traders.

Overleaf: Metal doll's house furnishings made by the German firm Schweizer, much rarer than wooden furniture but less agreeable.

were imported. The English dolls were stylised, the German ones more naturalistic, but none could be described as cuddly and many were clearly made for an adult market. The wooden dolls were usually opulently and extravagantly clothed, and the main pleasure for children was in clothing and unclothing dolls.

The simple skittle-shaped dolls lasted well into the nineteenth century, and Queen Victoria's own dolls were of this type. She had 132, dressed and undressed 32, and left the others to her governess. Dolls for the better-off came with many changes of clothes and a range of accessories, such as fans and hand-bags. Wooden dolls competed directly with papier mâché dolls, made from a paper pulp, fortified with a variety of ingredients, and surprisingly strong (in the Victorian period a piano was made of papier mâché). Eighteenth-century composition dolls are usually moulded to waist level, with leather used for the lower limbs. Not many have survived because they are inclined to flake unless they are lacquered (as papier-mâché furniture and trays are), and, often because of the added ingredients, are eaten by insects.

Some of these dolls are splendidly made, and there was a good deal

of innovation, such as the fitting of bamboo teeth. As with wooden toys, the makers are mostly anonymous. Wax dolls were made in ancient times, and dolls of wax were sold in fourteenth-century Venice. Wax was a good material, as colouring on wax (mostly beeswax though a Brazilian wax was sometimes added as well as turpentine)) produced a lifelike complexion, and there were also skilled practitioners. Wax portraits were common in the eighteenth century, exhibited at the Royal Academy, but the doll-makers were craftsmen adept in making wax effigies of dead children who could use their skills in a less morbid way. Early wax dolls were solid, but the "poured wax" method proved more effective; wax was poured into moulds, removing most of the wax in the core before it set, so the poured wax doll was hollow, with the exception of hands and feet, though often only the heads were of wax. Bodies were not regarded as important as they would be covered by clothes.

There are two main names in poured wax dolls, Montanari and Pierotti. Madame Montanari exhibited at the Great Exhibition of 1851 to much acclaim, but apparently she disappeared from sight in

Above: Two dolls' house chairs, one wood, the other painted lead and fabric, and a wood and glass bead settee, all late-nineteenth century.

Opposite: Two of the most famous dolls in the antique world, Lord and Lady Clapham, made of wood, fairly crudely carved, but lavishly dressed.

1887, though the Pierotti family continued making wax dolls until 1935. Lifelike portrait dolls were made, and Pierotti also did Old Testament figures for what market one can only puzzle. Children could send samples of their own hair to be planted in the skulls of custom-made wax dolls. Wax was also used over papier mâché.

Wax could not compete with china, especially unglazed porcelain known as bisque, and in this field the French were supreme, though the Germans entered the market and eventually became the dominant force as their organization and marketing were far superior. After the Franco-Prussian War when the French were soundly beaten and humiliated the French doll-makers were psychologically unable to fight back and contended themselves with sneering at the German dolls. Their own dolls, they claimed were thoroughly French.

Early china dolls date from around 1830, but production rose and from about 1845 china dolls became very popular, more robust than wax and less liable to be chewed by their owners. Glazed china dolls are puffy and unglamorous, but the makers of bisque dolls created the classic collectable doll, accumulating expertise, making more sophisticated joints, and incorporating a variety of gadgetry, such as "Mama" and "Papa" sounds, musical boxes in the base, internal springs to connect the limbs and make them movable in a realistic way, and increasingly efficient ways of opening and closing the eyes. This was usually done by lead weights.

The classic French doll of bisque was known as a *Parisienne*, so perfect that many were mannequins rather than dolls and were used for window display of high couture. And for almost the first time dolls were made as very young children, and these proved a great success. The *bébés* developed into the character dolls, where young children were posed in naturalistic attitudes, crawling, sleeping, and being

Above: An early doll's house of about 1800 with original contents and wallpaper, rare in any case but rarer still because no-one has had the impulse to update the contents, or at least if so, it has been done unobtrusively.

Opposite: The Scribe, an automaton by the celebrated maker Pierre Jaquet-Droz and made in 1770, would be a delight to any child who got his or her hands on it and cause panic to any right-feeling adult. The Scribe did not only seem to write but actually did write.

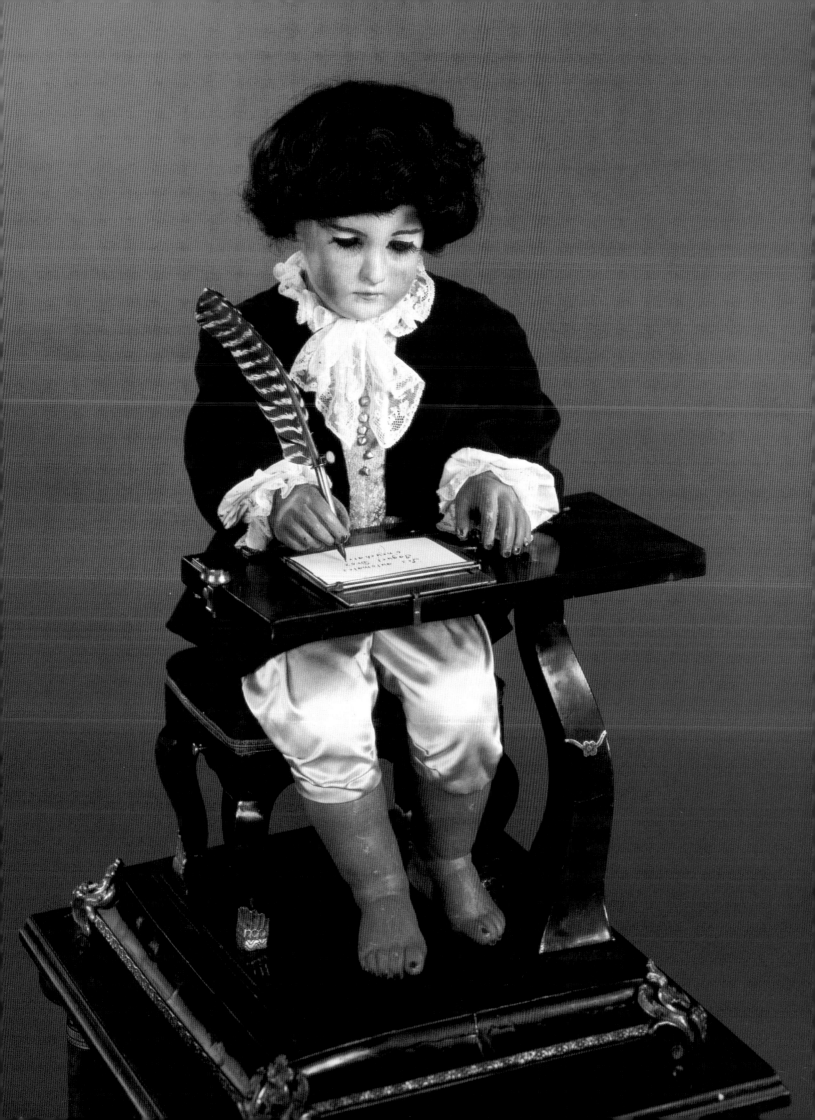

Above: An animated musical Victorian Christmas party.

Opposite: An American walking doll with carriage. The problem of walking dolls was always a poser, often solved by having the dolls on wheels under a long dress. Dolls with moving legs commonly fell over, though the French in particular made many attempts for the massive Parisian doll market.

cute or naughty. It opened the way to a somewhat glutinous sentimentality, reaching its peak in the American "Kewpies" (a corruption of Cupid), in 1913. Parian china was also fashionable for a period; Parian is a white slightly glazed porcelain imitating marble, but it was hardly suited to doll-making, and not surprisingly the emphasis of Parian dolls was on the haughty and the imperious where the underlying stark white would not be out of place. It was the most stylish of materials and many dolls were modelled on real people. It dates from the 1850s and was at its peak for about 30 years.

Except in wax, the British doll-industry had been unenterprising, and few of the major porcelain factories even ventured into a profitable market, though Worcester was as good as any and better than most. It was far easier just to import French dolls.

In America, the situation was just the same. The first American patent for a doll's head was registered in 1858 to Ludwig Greiner of Philadelphia. This was made of composition, and American jointed wooden dolls were not on the market until 1873, when the format was virtually obsolescent, though the jointing was superior to that of Germany and dolls could be twisted into any position and stay there. They also had the ability to stand up, rare in wooden dolls, where

legs were sometimes replaced by a circular hoop, covered with a voluminous skirt. The Americans also developed metal hands and feet, comparatively rare in Europe.

A characteristic of classic French dolls is that the faces are often plump and prosperous. They were stylised, rather reminiscent of the Queen Anne types though much more appealing, though this appeal owes much to the marvellous costuming, invariably hand-sewn by ill-paid seamstresses on outwork who had unimaginable skills and are the unsung heroines of the business. The more industrious owners made the clothes themselves.

French dolls are dominated by a handful of figures, especially Jumeau and Bru, sometimes difficult to differentiate. Jumeau employed 1,000 workers in 1889 and claimed to be selling 300,000 dolls a week. Jumeau moulds went walkabout, and a number of fakes using these moulds are still on the market. The Japanese were particularly clever at producing *Parisienne* fakes. To counter the German threat, Jumeau, Bru and the other French doll-makers went into business together and formed the *Société de Fabrication des Bébés et Jouets*, but this amalgamation was a confession of defeat even though it produced millions of dolls.

German makes included the most prolific, Marseille, Kämmer and Reinhardt (established 1886), Simon and Halbig, and Heubach. The Germans were particularly adept at character dolls, and were copied by the French. But the most significant factor in doll-making was the burgeoning if at first slow-moving American industry, skilled in advertising and promotion and whose mail-order operation was unique in the world. "Billikin" of 1909 with a "Can't Break 'Em Head" of composition was a market leader, and within a few months was on sale in England. Although half the dolls in America were German in 1914, World War I gave great opportunities to British and American toy-makers, whose pseudo-German bisque dolls were poor, and for several years after the war ended in 1918 there was a reluctance to import German dolls.

The "Billikin" was typical of a new attitude towards dolls. It was advertised with the slogan:

> I'm Billikin whose lucky grin,
> Makes gloom fly out and joy run in,
> I'm fond of little boys and girls
> I love to nestle 'gainst their curls.

An interest feature of this is that boys as well as girls were being targeted, though it was the parents who reacted to the advertising offensive, and bought and bought and bought. Due to its appearance in books by the creator of the gollywog, the old fashioned brightly coloured wooden peg doll became fashionable, and soft toys such as teddy bears were made in their millions. The advertising was clever and often misleading, but it worked, and as the new unbreakable dolls were astonishingly cheap (in Britain 45/- (£2.25) a dozen, in the US even less) they were disposable. There was also a resurgence in rag dolls, and in the 1920s cinema cartoon characters such as Mickey Mouse and Goofy competed with tin-plate toys and usually won out.

Britain had its own superb soft-toy industry, though German toys continued to be imported on account of their cheapness (though the economic chaos of Germany had its effect) . The U.S. and Britain had seen off the German monopoly. The best-selling rag doll of the twentieth century is the Cabbage Patch doll which has its own band of dedicated collectors.

Catering for a slightly different market were dolls' houses, formerly called babies' houses, sometimes called cabinets. These were originally adults' toys made for the rich, constructed by estate carpenters. The earliest dolls' house is sixteenth century, but they did not become truly popular until the eighteenth. In the nineteenth century they reached

Above: "Noddies", heads on stems slotting into a torso, were once very common, but they are rarely seen today and yet are amazingly inexpensive. This one is modelled as an itinerant toy seller, and is German of the last quarter of the nineteenth century.

Opposite: Dean's was one of the major British toy makers and they produced their version of Mickey Mouse in velvet.

Imagerie D'Epinal

Opposite: Two clockwork nodding dolls.

Above: A French toy theatre of the late-nineteenth century, far more "classical" in appearance than the British toy theatres.

Above: Steiff is the most sought-after maker of Teddy bears, characterised by a tab on one ear and a slightly humped back. If they are out of the ordinary, such as these skittle bears, they can command very high prices from the multitude of Teddy bear collectors.

their peak, often made by hobbyists who forgot to put in windows, had stairs which lead nowhere, and had hidden rooms which no-one would ever see. Access was by a lift-off roof or a door behind. Some large houses were replicas of real houses. There was intense enthusiasm in furnishing them and filling them with miniature dolls, usually out of scale. Dolls' houses are invariably claustrophobic, often quite mad.

Children's dolls' houses, often made of card though wood remained predominant, catered for the pleasure in multi-element toys such as Noah's arks, toy soldiers, zoos and menageries and train sets. There were also toy food shops, with miniature corn-flake packets, tiny packets of tea, toy post offices with minute stationery, and model theatres, which date from about 1800. Characters were made of card and were pushed along slots in the stage. Toy theatre was popular until the early twentieth century when real cinema made them obsolete almost overnight. America relied heavily on imported toy theatres until 1870. There was a huge market for toy-theatre plays – one of the first American playlets was "The Fiend of the Rocky Mountain" which gives some idea of children's taste of the time.

A MARVELLOUS DOLL.

A PRIMA DONNA

In Every Home.

SOMETHING NEW. The picture represents the wonderful **Webber Singing Doll**, *just out*, and the GREATEST NOVELTY *ever offered in Children's Toys.* The Doll itself is of the finest French make, with WAX HEAD, REAL HAIR, and finest eyes, and is no different in appearance from the best of imported dolls; but within its body is a most ingenious machine, which, when it is lightly pressed, causes the Doll to sing one of the following airs: "*Home, sweet home,*" "*Greenville,*" "*I want to be an angel,*" "*There is a happy land,*" "*Sweet bye and bye,*" "*Bonnie Doon,*" "*How can I leave thee?*" "*A B C Song,*" "*America,*" "*Thou, thou reign'st*" (German), "*Frohe Botschaft*" (German), "*Tell Aunt Rhoda,*" "*Buy a broom,*" "*Yankee Doodle.*" The singing attachment is **a perfect musical instrument,** finely made, and will not get out of order, and *the doll is sold for the same price that toy dealers ask for the same quality of a doll without the singing attachment.* Walking and talking dolls have been made, but at high prices, and liable to get quickly out of order, and they do not afford the little ones half the enjoyment that our wonderful Singing Doll does. We have two sizes. **No. 1.—** 22 inches high, wax head, real hair, fine eyes, and a very beautiful face—a strictly first-class quality French Doll. Price, complete, **$2.75. No. 1½.** —Same as No. 1, but eyes close when laid down. **50c.** extra. **No. 2.—**30 inches high, extra fine wax head, real hair, and finest eyes. Price, **$5.00. No. 2½.**—Same as No. 2, but with closing eyes. **75c.** extra. *These prices include boxing and packing.* Sent to any address on receipt of price. An embroidered chemise, not shown in engraving, goes with each Doll. ☞These prices are as low as the same quality doll is generally sold at without the Singing Attachment. It is the most beautiful present that can be made to a child, and will afford more amusement than any other toy in the market. THE TRADE SUPPLIED. Address the MASSACHUSETTS ORGAN COMPANY, 57 Washington Street, Boston, Mass., U.S.A.

Left: New technology, such as the introduction of the phonograph and gramophone, gave dolls the opportunity to talk and sing (after a fashion) rather than emit "mama" sounds. This was promoted largely by the American toy makers. It was not wholly successful and was a short-lived novelty.

Below: The Edison talk doll had the advantage of being promoted by one of the world's greatest entrepreneurs but even he could not establish it as a standard line. High technology and cuddliness did not match.

WE ARE NOW PREPARED
TO SUPPLY THE

EDISON
TALKING
DOLL

EDISON'S
TALKING DOLL.

TO THE TRADE
ONLY.

For Wholesale Price and Terms, Address

EDISON PHONOGRAPH TOY MFG. CO.,
No. 138 FIFTH AVENUE,
NEW YORK.

BOARD GAMES AND CARDS

The value of board games and card games to society has never been fully appreciated. To dismiss them as mere pastimes is to miss the point. Their appeal is to both adults and children, and many games such as "Monopoly" span the age gap. There are board games depending on chance ("Snakes and Ladders"), on chance and skill ("Cluedo"), and skill (chess and draughts).

They serve a number of functions; they ease the wheels of social life as in whist drives, they are shared activities for parents and their children, and, often overlooked, they channel aggression, for the aim, hidden or not, is to win. Just as some sports are surrogates for war (sometimes resembling war), so board and card games are a form of stylised confrontation. They are also educational, and although this was the main reason for their introduction in large numbers in the eighteenth and nineteenth centuries, it is rarely one of the features of more recent games. Sometimes the urge to win can be stifled – as when an adult is playing board games or cards with a young child, and only the most high-minded and benevolent can do this with great enjoyment, the self-imposed constraint offset by the pleasure the child gets when winning.

Board games go back at least to the ancient civilizations, and beautifully made boards have been excavated in Rome and Greece, though what games were played is often difficult to work out beyond the fact that they were complex, though probably not so much as the ancient Chinese game mah jong, a game only known in the west since 1923

Above: Board games were popular with the ancient Romans and quite a large number survive, though often without any indication how they were played, though this one has its counters.

Opposite: A weighted Staunton ivory chess set of about 1860. Staunton was not the maker but a chess player who established what is still the standard design for chess pieces.

Above: A gaming board made from shell and lapis lazuli of the second millenium BC and originating in Mesopotamia.

Opposite: Venetian playing cards from 1758. Playing cards were brought to Europe from the East in the fourteenth century. The modern 52-card pack was evolved in France in the sixteenth century.

when mah jong became a craze amongst the smart set. It is played with 136 or 144 tiles.

Playing cards were intended for adults, though up to the eighteenth century children freely participated. In the Victorian period it is said that card-playing amongst the young was discouraged as encouraging them in vice, but this would only apply to a small section of the middle classes and there is no reason to believe that it was less popular amongst children though a host of card games for children such as "Happy Families" were issued. Many of these games were fashioned on simple card games such as snap, and the first of the card word games made their appearance. These games, such as the 1930s "Lexicon" (a laid-out game similar to the much later "Scrabble" except with cards instead of tiles, and thus taking up an inordinate amount of table space) became very popular.

The origin of playing cards is vague. They were not used by the Greeks or Romans, and it has been argued that they originated in the East and were brought to Europe by Arab traders. Their use in Europe may be positively dated to 1377 when Johannes, a German monk, wrote: "... a certain game called the game of cards has come

112

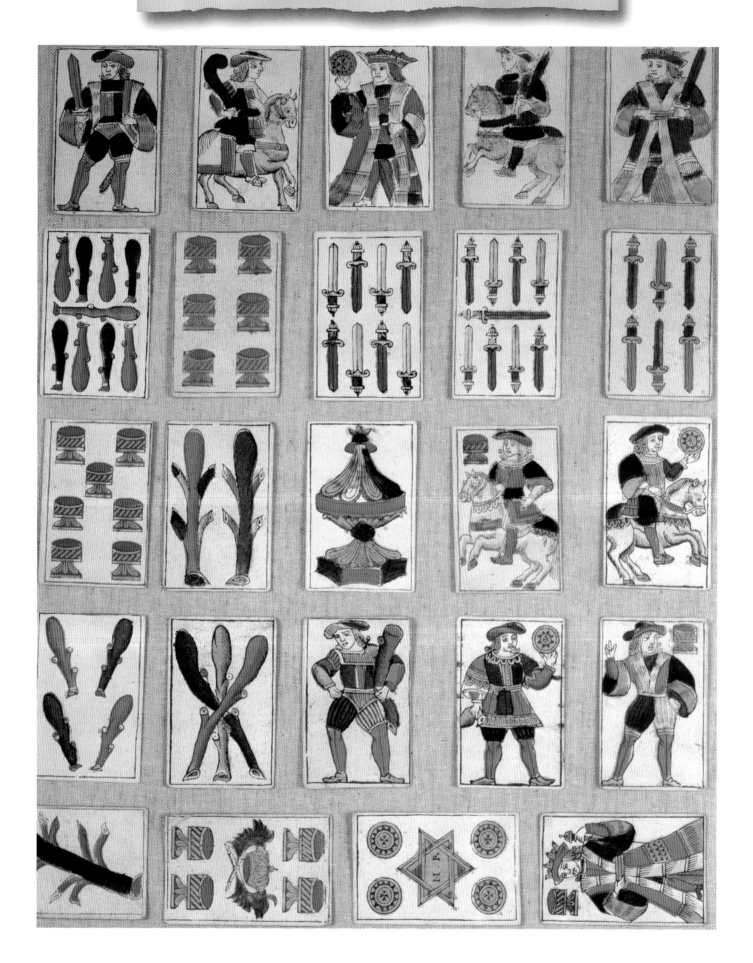

Above: A board game from Thebes in Egypt dating from 1200/1300 BC.

to us in this year". After the fourteenth century playing cards are frequently mentioned in manuscripts.

The earliest cards were hand-painted, often beautifully, and although the European pack always had four suits they bore innumerable names. One of the earliest surviving German packs c 1440 had Falcons, Hounds, Herons, and Lures (used to recall the falcon). Wood-block printing, invented in Germany, enabled playing cards to be produced for the masses. In France the suits were called *coeurs* (hearts), *piques* (pikes), *carreaux* (paving tiles), and *trèfles* (trefoils). Diamonds, hearts, spades and clubs were evolved from a sixteenth-century design from Rouen.

There are two cards of card games: those involving the collection of like cards or runs such as rummy, or those where the object is to take tricks, such as whist. In India, traditional Hindu cards were circular; in China, playing cards were in packs of 120, and date from the T'ang Dynasty (611 – 906), though the Chinese had other card games based on dominoes.

Card-playing in Britain reached its peak in the eighteenth century and Edmond Hoyle (1672 – 1769) was its chronicler and grey eminence, giving lessons and writing on whist, the main card game. "According to Hoyle" is still a catchphrase, though decreasingly so as history goes remorselessly down the drain. Bridge, the card game with the most cachet, was not invented until 1886, and was developed from whist.

Left: Tarot is the oldest form of card game, and with its enigmatic and curious designs it is used for fortune-telling. This Italian pack is engraved and hand coloured.

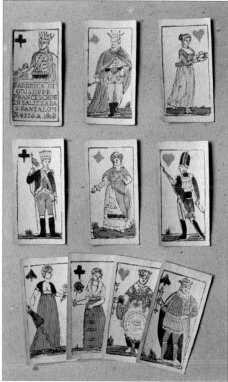

Above: Picture cards from a pack of playing cards of the eighteenth century.

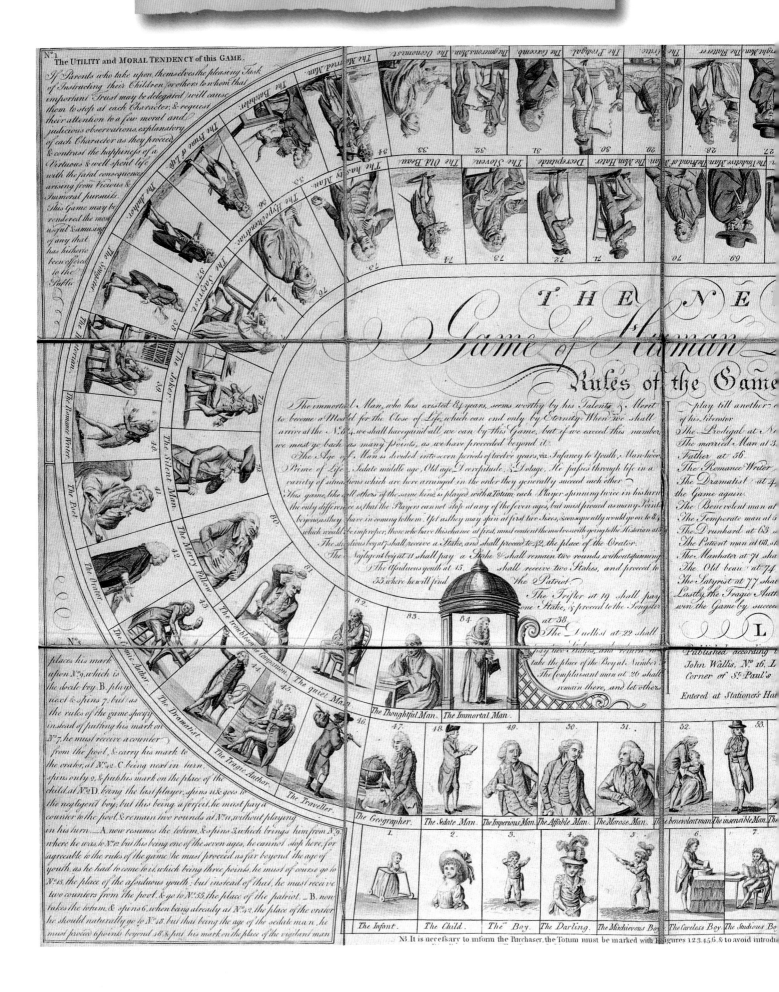

This Game may be played by any number of
Persons at a time; but care must be taken, that
each player make use of a different mark to
move with, & be provided with at least
twelve counters each, & agree how
much to value them per dozen.
Let us then suppose that four
Gentlemen agree to play a
game together, & stake
four counters each.
A takes red for his
mark,—B green,
C black, and
D white.
A begins &
spins 9, &
accordingly

...s to take his place, and then he shall go back to the place

...er 30 shall pay four Stakes, & go back to the Careless boy at 6.

...all receive two Stakes for his Wife's Portion and go to be a good

...40 shall pay two Stakes & go back to the mischievous Boy at 5.

...all pay four Stakes to the Masters of his Art, and shall begin

...shall go to 78, to amuse himself with the Joker.—

...ll go to 82, to find the Quiet man

...ll pay two Stakes, and go back to the Child at 2.

...receive two Stakes & go to amuse himself with the merry fellow at 80.

...ay two Stakes, and go back to the Obstinate youth at 16.

...ll receive one Stake, and let each of the others play one round.

...ay four Stakes, and go back to the Malignant boy at 6.

...t 45 shall go to the place of the Immortal Man at 84, and

...him.

LONDON.

...ct of Parliament July 14. 1790, by

...ate Street, and E. Newbery, the

...rch Yard.

The figures around the board (partial, as legible):

The Complaisant Man. — The Dressy Man — The Flying Man — The Dissembler — The Duellist — The Player — The Lover — The Miser — The Drunkard — The Philosopher — The Libertine — The Gallant — The Obstinate Youth — The Rebellious Youth — The Old Man — The Glutton — The Ambitious Man — The Temperate Man — The Volunteer — The Youth — The Negligent Boy — The Thoughtless Boy — The Good Father — The Docile Boy — The Patriot — The Malignant Boy — The Brute — The Learned Man — The Gambler

...being
...some again
...he spins 11,
...comes in N°,
...the place of the
...Volunteer, where
...he now leaves his
...mark. D, having
...thrown in before, must
...as already said, remain
...at N°n, this round & the
...next without playing. thus
A being next in turn, & at N°55
...spins 3, which would bring him to
N°58, but according to the rules of the
game he must pass on to N°8 & pull his
mark on the place of the quiet man.—B
...spins again, & fetches 9, which, being at N°54
...would naturally bring him to 63, but according to
the rules of the game) he must go back to the place of
the child at N°2. & pay two counters to the pool.—C, who
...is now at N°13, spins 6, which would naturally bring him to
N°19, but instead of stopping at this last number according to the
rules of the game) he pays a counter to the pool, & goes to the place of
the songster at N°38. D, must as already mentioned also remain this round
...ood playing. A again takes the totum spins 5 & being before at N°82, compleats N°84, takes
the pla...C the immortal man & wins the game.

Until the end of the nineteenth century playing cards had square corners. It is a far cry to the early card games intended for children with their religious and educational overtones. "Authors, their Birth Place and Fame" would not have been much fun, nor would have been the "Royal Historical Game of cards", 45 cards with portraits of kings and queens of England. The Americans had begun to make their own children's cards in the early nineteenth century, and in 1845 issued "The New Impenetrable Secret or (or should it be "of"?) Young Ladies" which sounds much more interesting than its English contemporaries though this and the "Gentleman's Polite Puzzle" proclaimed their promulgation of "virtue and modesty".

With "Happy Families" and its ilk came a relaxation, games such as "Word Making and Word Taking" were intended for adults and children. "Bargains", "Fairy Tales", "Circulating Library", "Zooloo" with circular cards "Cheating" (no doubt very useful) and "Psycho, a weird and wonderful fortune-telling game" made their appearances, as well as others to teach musical notation ("Musical Notes") and another, "The Stock Exchange", presumably to teach children how to make millions.

Except for "Happy Families" none of these games lasted very long,

Above: The backs of cards vary enormously, and playing cards can provide a diverse and inexpensive collection. This set of the Queen Anne period depicts the queen, the Duke of Marlborough and scenes from his victorious battles.

Opposite: A walrus ivory Russian chess set of the late-eighteenth century. Walrus ivory is regarded as greatly inferior to the ivory from elephant trunks with little tangible reason. Chess was, and is, a passion of the Russians who have produced a high proportion of world champions.

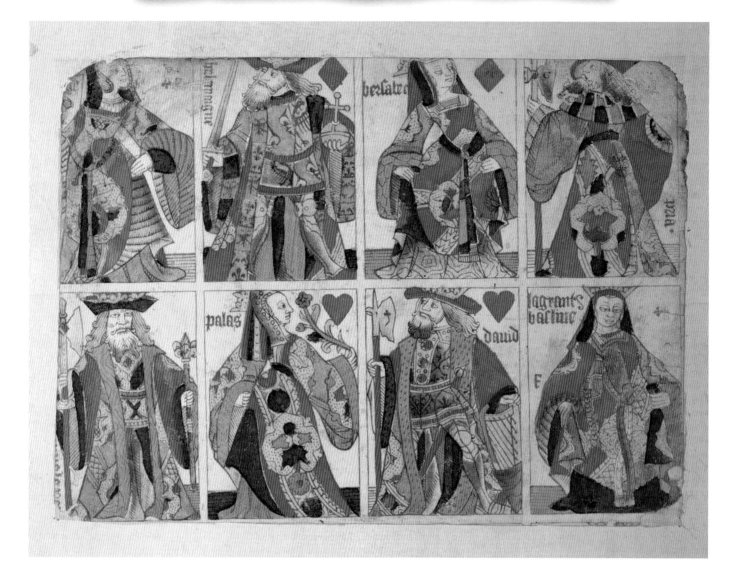

Above: Uncut playing cards from the late eighteenth-century.

as the potential was lacking, but they were cheap to make and easy to promote through colourful packaging. Their popularity went into decline when children of the twentieth century were offered a wider variety of leisure pursuits.

Said to be the earliest dated board game, "A Journey Through Europe or the Play of Geography" was printed in 1759. By the throw of a teetotum, the player proceeds from York to London by way of Iceland, the Baltic, and the continent of Europe with a brief excursion to Siberia (sic!) in the top right hand corner of the map. Many of these early board games have survived because they were cut into sections, usually twelve or sixteen, and mounted on stout linen, then folded, like touring maps. Good quality paper was always used, and the designs were from engraved plates. They were then hand coloured.

Opposite: Jigsaw puzzles derive from educational "dissected maps" first produced in the 1760s, and pure entertainment jigsaws did not arrive in quantity until the jigsaw was invented in the nineteenth century. Early favourites were Biblical scenes, such as the history of Joseph.

The most famous of these early games is "The Game of Goose". It predates 1759 as it is referred to in the copious rules to the journey through Europe game, and was sufficiently well-known to be quoted by Oliver Goldsmith in his poem *The Deserted Village*:

> The Pictures plac'd for ornament and use,
> The Twelve good rules, the royal game of Goose

Above: An apparently very early - and somewhat frayed - playing card of indeterminate date.

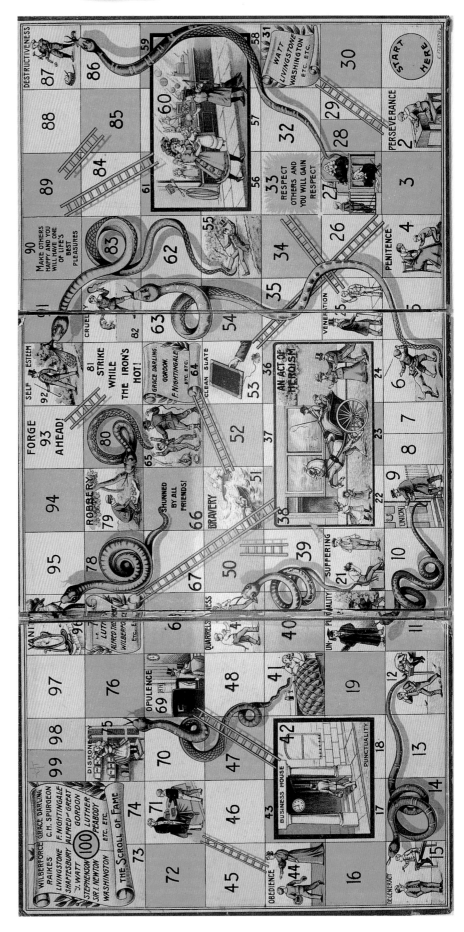

Right: Snakes and ladders is one of the best known of board games, and this German example of about 1900 is of the traditional type. The ups and downs of life provided an impetus for many "improving" board games.

The vast majority of games are "progression" games, governed by the throw of a dice or a teetotum. In "the Game of Goose" there are 63 spaces, the player starts from a corner, and works his or her way in. Some are circular or oval, and in the form of a helix so that the player gradually winds round and round until getting to the centre. The pictures are elaborate, and so well-drawn that competent artists must have been involved. In his catalogue of 1813 called "Amusing Publications for the Improvement of Youth" one of the best-known makers, John Wallis, advertised 33 games including "The New Game of Human Life", "Universal History and Chronology" and "British Sovereigns". These were sold for many decades, and the British sovereigns were updated in 1837 to include Queen Victoria.

There were board games about arithmetic, mythology, and astronomy. All had a strong moral tone. In the game on astronomy the player could well land in the County Gaol "the place for those who attend to the motions of Billiard Balls, more than to the motions of the Planets". One of the earliest board games for amusement is "The Magic Ring" (1796), which could be played by any number of players up to "18 or more". As the board was of average size it must have all been very congested.

Above: Happy Families was probably the most popular children's card game. Here a pack is accompanied by a calendar and scraps, either for a scrap book or for a screen.

The game-makers, predominant amongst which was William Spooner, kept up to date with current events – "The Railway Game" was issued about 1839. It is estimated that about 200 board games were published between 1750 – 1850, and the Great Exhibition of 1851 devoted a whole section to such amusements. From about 1839 lithography was used for colouring board games, but hand-painted games continued into the 1870s. The rules were always tedious and long-winded, and when America imported the geographical games and adapted them for American "travellers" the makers continued to use the same kind of lengthy instructions.

Below: The Misfitz card game of the 1920s featuring Alice in Wonderland characters. There is only a certain amount of variation possible in children's card games, most covered by snap and Happy Families and their derivatives.

It was only in the present century that true toy-makers rather than "geographers " (map-makers) and booksellers began to remodel board games by providing them with a minimum of rules and providing bright colour for their updated versions of "Snakes and Ladders" and more enjoyable games than the throw-and-move type. Players had to make decisions in games such as "Ludo" rather than submit to the will of a thrown dice or teetotum. With the more modern games such as "Monopoly" the designing was crisp and appealing, far removed from the jam-packed muddle of nineteenth-century board games. Post-war board games, such as *Attaque*, demand more from the player, and frequently the market is the adult rather than the child.

"Dissected maps" were evolved in the 1760s to teach geography. We know them as jigsaw puzzles. The shapes were simple and few, and this was true when other designs were used, first of all educational and improving, and later for amusement. The jigsaw puzzles paralleled the board games as they were made by the same firms. The railway jigsaw and the railway game came out the same time. Mahogany and cedar gave way to pine, the invention of the jigsaw in the 1870s made the shapes more interesting and unorthodox, and in 1917 the use of plywood made jigsaw puzzles cheap, ingenious, and with an

immense range of subjects, especially when colour photographs began to be used. The cheapest jigsaw puzzles were made from card.

Not so dissimilar from jigsaw puzzles were picture blocks, cubes with a different fragment of a picture on each face so that assembling them offers a mild challenge. They were probably first made in the early nineteenth century, but no-one can be absolutely certain and early ones are rare, as, like jigsaw puzzle pieces, odd cubes are lost and the others are thrown away. Unlike dolls, few board games were cherished and valued, all children's card games eventually lost a card or two or became mixed up with other card games and were eventually dumped with exasperation. There are few classics, and many are unutterably boring.

Table games were produced in some quantity, and include tiddly-winks, shooting games in which discs are propelled towards a target by means of an elastic band, cricket games, lotto (bingo), horse-racing games, aeroplane, train, and car games, games where marbles are rolled down a chute into sockets, bagatelle, but few famous firms with the exception of Chad Valley of Birmingham were involved, and most table games were ephemeral. As with so many multiple-element toys pieces became lost, and table games were discarded without cere-mony. They are a neglected area on the fringes of the antique world, but they are often shoddily made, very few have much age, and those that have survived rouse little interest except amongst those whose desire is to collect something no-one else wants.

Above: An English spelling alphabet in bone dating from about 1800.

INDEX